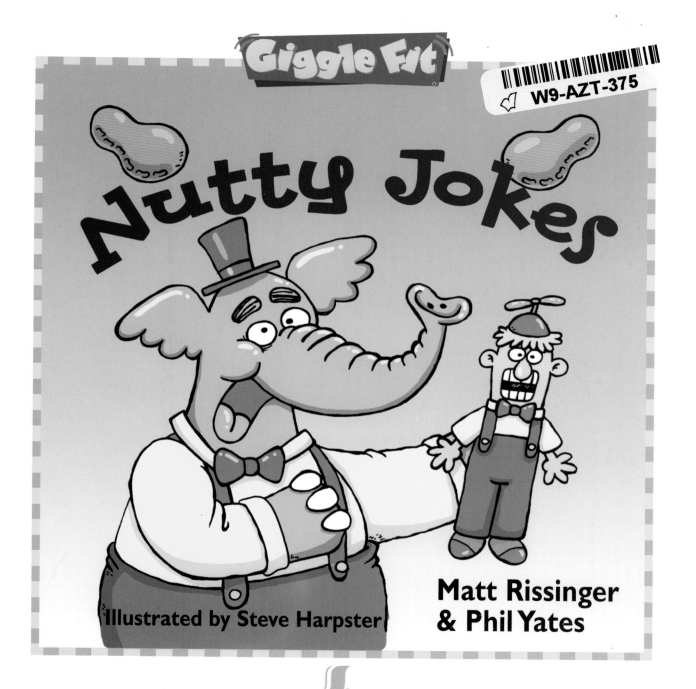

Giggle Fit

Nutty Jokes

Illustrated by Steve Harpster

Matt Rissinger
& Phil Yates

Sterling Publishing Co., Inc. New York

Library of Congress Cataloging-in-Publication Data

10   9   8   7   6   5   4   3   2   1

First paperback edition published in 2002 by
Sterling Publishing Company, Inc.
387 Park Avenue South, New York, N.Y. 10016
© 2001 by Matt Rissinger and Phil Yates
Distributed in Canada by Sterling Publishing
C/o Canadian Manda Group, One Atlantic Avenue, Suite 105
Toronto, Ontario, Canada M6K 3E7
Distributed in Great Britain and Europe by Chris Lloyd at Orca
Book Services, Stanley House, Fleets Lane, Poole BH15 3AJ, England
Distributed in Australia by Capricorn Link (Australia) Pty. Ltd.
P.O. Box 704, Windsor, NSW 2756 Australia

Printed in China

Sterling   ISBN 0-8069-8016-8   Hardcover
           ISBN 1-4027-0120-9   Paperback

What's big and white and lives in the Sahara Desert?
A lost polar bear.

What's a polar bear's favorite vacation spot?
Brrrr-muda.

What cartoon animal
weighs the least?
Skinny the Pooh.

What's brown and has 8 legs and a big trunk?
A spider coming home from a trip.

What kind of flowers would you give an absent-minded squirrel?
Forget-me-nuts.

What's an owl's favorite mystery?
A whooo-dunit.

What is a woodpecker's favorite kind of joke?
A knock-knock.

What would you call a lion that writes snappy songs?

King of the Jingle.

What would you get if you crossed a baby kangaroo with a TV buff?

A pouch potato.

What would you get if you crossed a guppy with a monkey?

A shrimpanzee.

Why don't fish go on-line?
Because they're afraid of being caught in the Net.

What kinds of doctors make fish look beautiful?
Plastic sturgeons.

What's an eel's favorite card game?
Glow Fish.

Where does a mother octopus shop for clothes for its children?
Squids 'R' Us.

What would you get if you crossed an octopus and a cat?
An animal with 8 arms and 9 lives.

Why did the turtle see a psychiatrist?
He wanted to come out of his shell.

What do cats use to keep their breath fresh?
Mouse wash.

What do baby cats wear?
Diapurrrrs.

How do you know when your cat's been on the Internet?
Your mouse has teeth marks in it.

What happened to the cat that swallowed a ball of wool?

It had mittens.

What do you call a cat with a pager?

A beeping tom.

What would you get if you crossed a cat with a porcupine?

An animal that goes "meowch" when it licks itself.

What did they name the dog
with the receding hairline?
Bald Spot.

What do you give a dog that
loves computers?
Doggie diskettes.

Why did the puppy go to the hair salon?
To get a shampoodle.

How do you turn a beagle into a bird?
Remove the B.

Why did the dog get a ticket?
For double barking.

What would you get if you
crossed a dog with a chicken?
Pooched eggs.

What dinosaur always came in third in Olympic events?

Bronze-to-saurus.

What dinosaur was at home on the range?

Tyrannosaurus Tex.

In what age did the Sloppy-o-saurus live?

The Messy-zoic period.

Why are dinosaurs healthier than dragons?
Because dinosaurs don't smoke.

What do dragons like
most about school?
The fire drills.

DRAGO the GREAT

Where do great dragons
end up?
In the Hall of Flame.

What's big and gray and weighs down the front of your car?
An elephant in the glove compartment.

How do you know when there's an elephant in your chocolate pudding?
When it's lumpier than usual.

How can you tell the age of an elephant?
Count the candles on its birthday cake.

How do you give an elephant a bath?

First you find a very large rubber duckie.

How many elephants does it take to program a computer?

Four. One to work the keyboard and three to hold down the mouse.

What would you get if you crossed a parrot and an elephant?

An animal that tells you everything it remembers.

What do snakes do after a fight?
They hiss and make up.

What is a snake's
favorite subject?
SSScience.

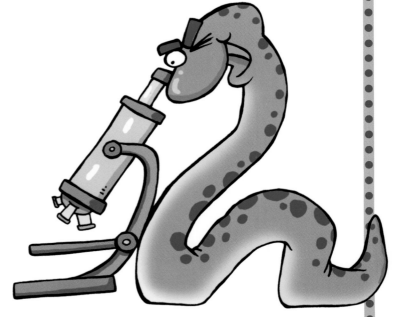

What kind of snake wears dark glasses and a
trench coat?
A spy-thon.

What would you get if you crossed a snake
with Bigfoot?
Ssss-quatch.

What would you call a
snake that drinks too
much coffee?
A hyper viper.

What would you get if you crossed an eight-foot snake
with a five-foot snake?
Nothing. Snakes don't have feet.

How do pigs store their computer files?
On sloppy disks.

Why did the computer squeak?
Because someone stepped on its mouse.

What do witches like to do on the computer?
Use the spell checker.

Why did the computer go to the eye doctor?
To improve its website.

What's a cat's favorite kind of computer?
A laptop.

What kind of computer mail do mice exchange?
Eeek-mail.

How do you make a cream puff?
Chase it around the block a few times.

What is a baker's favorite kind of book?
A who-donut.

What dessert can you eat in the ocean?
Sponge cake.

Why did the banana go
to the hospital?
It didn't peel so good.

What did cavemen eat
for lunch?
Club sandwiches.

What's the pizza maker's motto?
Cheesy come, cheesy go.

Where do sheep buy their clothes?
Lamb shops.

Where do spies do their shopping?
At the snooper market.

What did the rip say to the pair of pants?
"Well, I'll be darned!"

Why does Superman wear such big shoes?
Because of his amazing feats.

What has four wheels and diaper rash?
   A baby in a shopping cart.

What did the tie say to the hat?
   "You go on ahead, I'll just hang around."

What do short-sighted ghosts wear?
Spook-tacles.

How do ghosts get to school?
On a ghoul bus.

What position did the
ghost play on the
soccer team?
Ghoulie.

Why didn't the skeleton go
to the ball?
**Because he had no body
to go with.**

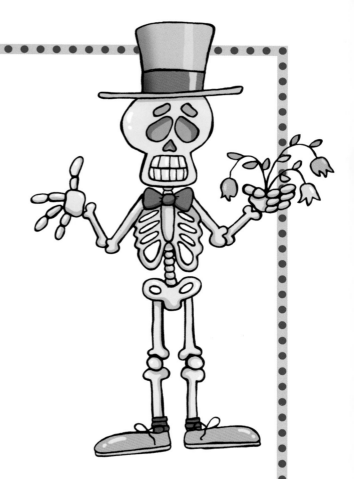

Why did the skeleton refuse
to bungee jump?
He didn't have any guts.

What would you get if you crossed nursery rhymes
with scary stories?
Mother Goosebumps.

What would you get if you crossed a vampire and a mummy?

Either a flying bandage or a gift-wrapped bat.

What do you call six vampires to go?

A Drac pack.

What would you get if you crossed a skunk with the Frankenstein monster?

Stinkenstein.

Why is it so hard to celebrate Father's Day in Egypt?
Because there are more mummies than daddies.

What was King Tut's favorite card game?
Gin Mummy.

What would you give King Kong for his birthday?
Anything he wants.

What was the butterfly's favorite subject?
Moth-ematics.

Why was the pony sent to the principal's office?
For horsing around.

Why was the chicken sent to the principal's office?
Because it kept pecking on the other kids.

What's dusty and gray
and goes "Cough-
cough!"
**An elephant cleaning
erasers.**

COUGH
HACK

What did the chalkboard
say to the eraser?
**"You rub me the
wrong way."**

What did the wad of gum say to the school desk?
"I'm stuck on you."

How did the flower do on the test?
It got all bees.

Why did the firefly do so
well on the test?
It was very bright.

What did the skeleton do before the big test?
It boned up.

Why did the cows get such low grades?
They copied off each udder.

Why did the squirrels get such low grades?
They drove the teacher nuts.

Why did the giant squids
get such low grades?
**They couldn't ink
straight.**

Why did King Kong wear a baseball glove to the airport?
He had to catch a plane.

Can kids learn to fly jet planes?
Yes, but they have to use training wheels.

What's gray, has 800 feet, and never leaves the ground?
An airplane full of elephants.

What kind of clothes do parachutists wear?
Jumpsuits.

Why don't dogs like to
travel on planes?
They get jet wag.

What would you get if you
crossed a blimp with an
orangutan?
A hot-air baboon.

What swings through the trees and tastes good with milk?
Chocolate chimp cookies.

What has a nice trunk but never goes on a trip?
A tree.

Why did the tree go to the hospital?
For a sap-endectomy.

Why did the Christmas
tree go to the hospital?
It had tinsel-itis.

What do trees watch on
television?
Sap operas.

What grows on trees and is scared of wolves?
The three little figs.

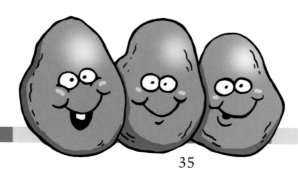

What do rabbits put on the backs of their cars?
Thumper stickers.

What kind of cars do rubber bands drive?
Stretch limos.

What did the little tire want to be when he grew up?
A big wheel.

What happens when a frog is double-parked on a lily pad?

It's toad away.

Why did the computer give up its car?

It was always crashing.

How come they never look for crooks in church?
Because crime doesn't pray.

What happened when the duck was arrested?
It quacked under pressure.

What did the security guard say to the firefly?
"Halt! Who glows there?"

What's yellow,
plastic, and holds
up banks?
A robber duckie.

Where do detectives sleep?
Under cover.

Why would Snow White make a great judge?
Because she is fairest of them all.

What would you get if you crossed a baseball player with a frog?
An outfielder who catches flies and then eats them.

Was the vampire race close?
Yes, it was neck and neck.

What kind of bee is always dropping the football?
A fumblebee.

At what sporting event can you find chicken and noodles?
The souper bowl.

What is a mummy's favorite sport?
Casketball.

What's a mouse's favorite sport?
Mice hockey.

What does a messy
flea need?
A lousekeeper.

What do videos do on their days off?
They unwind.

What would you get if you crossed a gardener
and a fortune teller?
Someone who weeds your palm.

What should you do if your smoke alarm goes off?
Run after it.

How do you keep your ears from ringing?
Get an unlisted head.

What should you do if you find Godzilla in your bed?
Sleep in the guest room.

Who protected King Arthur's castle from illegal break-ins?
The knight watchman.

Where did King Arthur keep his armies?
In his sleevies.

What didn't King Arthur ever get served at the Round Table?
A square meal.

Did you hear about the King Arthur stamp?
It's for over-knight delivery.

What do you call a sorceress with a broken broom?
A witchhiker.

What do witches wear to bed?
Fright-gowns.

What do witches say when they cast the wrong spell?
"Hexcuse me!"

How many witches does it take to change a lightbulb?
Just one — but she changes it into a toad.

What animal goes "Baa-Baa-Woof"?
A sheepdog.

Where do cows stay when they go on a trip?
In moo-tels.

What did one mule
say to the other mule?
**"I get a kick out
of you."**

What did the rooster say when he saw
Humpty Dumpty fall?
"Crack-a-doodle-doo."

How do pigs say goodbye?
With hogs and kisses.

INDEX